Trouble Sleeping? Evolve your spirituality

Yenni Payeski

Published by Yenni Payeski, 2021.

Also by Yenni Payeski

Problemas para dormir. Rituales y oraciones para que duermas más feliz
Trouble Sleeping? Evolve your spirituality
Acompañamiento espiritual por ruptura amorosa
Descodificación biológica Infantil
BIOLOGICAL DECODING. Children's Books

Watch for more at https://sentirseamada.com/.

Trouble Sleeping?

Evolve your spirituality

YENNI PAYESKI

Copyright © 2020 Author: Yenni Payeski

2nd edition, May 2021

Thank you,
Mom, for your immense love;
Kieran, my loving husband, for supporting me in this adventure;
Dad, for the simplicity of your heart;
Maga, Guille and Alex, for being my sources of learning and union.

Before starting

Are you part of the 60% of the population who has trouble sleeping several nights a week? If so, you should know that sleeping well is essential for your body to be protected against and optimally respond to any infection.

Understanding the signals that your body sends you about your spiritual, physical, and emotional state makes it possible to improve your sleeping cycle and sleep restfully.

If you...

usually wake up at dawn and go through episodes of interrupted sleep;

want to 'wake up feeling rested', 'sleep deeply to relax the mind' and 'have a pleasant sleep';

need to get rid of unhealthy habits and manage your emotions to improve your spiritual health and general well-being

... then I want to share some ancestral spiritual wisdom intertwined with modern knowledge to help you discover the benefits of good sleep and have a restorative experience.

The key to all this is sleep hygiene and cleansing of the heart.

Your nighttime habits can transform your life. That is why, with this book, I want to guide you towards inner tranquility so that you can rest with your heart free of worry.

I will help you make an internal analysis of your day and observe every moment you went through, whom you met, how they looked at you, and how you felt. I will give you the tools to find peace before you fall asleep and enter a deep process of inner strengthening.

The world needs you to sleep happily and to unveil the unique talents within you. To do this, you must connect with the love of God and become aware of your value before Him.

Take a deep breath and imagine

Imagine that you are in the middle of a very thick jungle. You look up and can barely glimpse the blue of the sky between the treetops. You hear the birds singing and recognize the sound of water running between some rocks. You try to identify where it is coming from because you know that you will be safe if you find the spring.

You decide to take the first steps towards the source, and your lips begin to feel the moisture as you get closer and closer to the water. You walk even faster, and you spot a smooth, crystalline stream. You kneel to one side and dip your hands in the spring. You feel deep inside the certainty that you will soon be secure.

Now you worry that the night is coming. But you already know which direction to take: follow the stream that will take you to the river and eventually to the sea. *Because that infinite source of life is God.*

We all want to find infinite love. There are many paths to reach the sea of wisdom where God dwells. No matter what one's spiritual or religious orientation might be. Because *He* is the only one who can expand our hearts. *He* is the only one that can guide us to a full life in the here and now.

For this, it is essential to adopt a comprehensive spiritual view of your daily life. This is the best way to recover restful practices that, for various reasons, we have forgotten.

Dare to discover

The content of this guide is simple but very important. You will improve your nighttime routine by developing practices for relief, rest, release, and heart hygiene so that you connect with your internal and ancestral wisdom.

I will help you optimize your night's rest so your mental acuity does not suffer. You will achieve emotional harmony and learn to maintain an ideal energy level throughout your day.

When we're tired, we tend to recall negative memories more than positive ones. And that's when pessimistic emotions take center stage. Thus, it becomes more difficult to be happy.

However, from a spiritual perspective, it is possible to return to a good sleep schedule. With time and practice, *meditation and centering prayer are reflected in the quality of your entire body's cells*, especially in your heart, the palace of the soul where your whole self is created.

The process of rediscovering restful sleep will be immensely beneficial to your heart and give way to new projects, new creativity – in short, a new life.

We will begin by assessing the life you are currently living. You will learn to recognize your emotions, thoughts, and desires and *look at your own story* as a creative force to observe, record, and honor your progress. These are powerful tools for self-knowledge and subsequent transformation.

Throughout the book, I will suggest meditations and questions that will allow you to get to know yourself better. Also, I will help you incorporate techniques into your daily routine, connect with your divine nature and innate tendency towards health and well-being.

Before proceeding, remember that the information available in this book is not intended to replace the advice of a professional physician. Always consult your doctor about any matter related to your health or the treatments and medicines you or those under your care take. This guide will simply accompany you in your experiential process.

Let me tell you my story

Hi, I'm Yenni Payeski.

I want to help you improve your daily routine, especially if you can't rest more than a couple of hours because your sleep is interrupted. My wish is that you get to know yourself through self-observation.

How did I get here?

From a very young age, I was interested in reading about spirituality. I still remember when I visited my grandfather Catalino and my grandmother Ana in Oberá, a small town in the North of Argentina known as the *mountain's capital*. I played among the vegetation and immerse myself in the streams and waterfalls hidden in the jungle. That's how I learned to enjoy nature. It was all fun and connection.

But when the sacred hour of the *siesta* arrived, everything stopped.

If you have never been to the North of Argentina, you should know that *the weather there is sweltering*. To beat the heat, people have a habit of sleeping after lunch, between 1:00 pm and 3:00 pm, when the weather is at its most stifling. This is an inviolable quiet time and has given rise to many legends that adults tell children to make them sleep.

Being a restless and curious girl, I could not sleep. Instead, I used those quiet hours to dive into my grandfather's thick yellow-leafed books *on spirituality and medicinal plants*.

Time went by and, like many women, I put my dreams aside as I grew up. I ended up graduating as an engineer and leading a very different life.

However, in my thirties, everything changed. At that time, I suffered from heartbreak and an immense feeling of loneliness. I soon developed an illness that led me to question the meaning of everything.

Lost and full of doubts, I decided to seek refuge in a spiritual retreat, something that would soon change my life – though I didn't know it back then.

During my retreat, I reconnected with my childhood experiences and found the company of God. When I returned home, I wanted to continue exploring the divine path. I signed up for a course on the minister of silence, listening, and reception. I also immediately began attending as many contemplative prayer retreats as I could. Little by little, thanks to the silence, I began to read again about what I was passionate about, and I no longer felt alone. I felt loved by God.

Every now and then, I still experience troubled nights, which are not easy to navigate. But, deep inside, I cling to the certainty that I am valuable and that everything shall pass. And so too shall that night. It is on me, Yenni, to decide how I want to proceed. Providence acts on me.

How did I decide to change?

I had spent an entire decade of my life in search of something that:
filled my heart ♥ *and made me feel whole;*
I truly liked;
allowed me to help other people;
I would enjoy without guilt;
made me happy.

I still remember it as if it were today. It was a Sunday in 2013.

It was infernally hot, and I decided to enter the Cathedral of Formosa to take refuge (or withdraw into myself, perhaps). I sat down on a bench and a few minutes later, a woman came up to me. She told me that she sang in the choir and, without further ado, invited me to participate in a charismatic prayer group for professionals.

At that time, I disbelieved in many things. I questioned myself and was convinced that religion was not for me. What was an engineer like me supposed to do in that place??? I was an executive of the financial system accustomed to calculating everything, to controlling everything. I was hiding in my unfounded prejudices.

However, something inside me told me that it would be different this time. Without overthinking it, I joined the prayer group the next day.

That Sunday in 2013, I started discovering the gifts that God had given me. The gifts that had always been there, respectfully waiting for me to find them.

But not everything was so easy for this girl from a small town. Soon after, I was offered a new promotion at work that required me to move to the great capital, Buenos Aires, some 600 miles from my hometown, Posadas.

It was not an easy decision, but my constant search for professional development led me to seize the opportunity. This option would also allow me to finally start a life project with the person I thought I loved. At thirty-three years old, I bet on love.

The ways God uses if we are dutiful can be wonderful. But this was not my case.

Shortly after this big decision, my relationship came to an end. I spent days crying and trying to hide my tears from other people. Sorrow took hold of me (although I wouldn't admit it). My projects had collapsed, and I felt I was going to die alone. My ego felt threatened.

I realized I could very well have been living in paradise and suffer just as much because I wasn't loved in the way I wanted. I was waiting for the wrong person. I was hoping someone else would give me what I couldn't give myself.

When I thought that I couldn't take it anymore, I drew strength from where I could and pushed myself towards transformation and love.

I moved again but decided to stay in the same challenging city, Buenos Aires. I discovered by searching on Google that I lived right by a spirituality center called Santa María. It was just five minutes away. Now if this isn't an example of an act of Divine Providence, I don't know what is!

I signed up for a course to become a spiritual companion at the center. During the five years of my studies, I underwent a profound transformation that reshaped who I was, and I found a new meaning for my life.

I managed to embark on my first trip alone, and I felt happy. I had learned to enjoy my solitude and the silence of the beach with just a book and a *mate* tea. For this experience, I had chosen the fantastic city of Miami, where I felt complete, master of my time and my life.

I traveled through beautiful parts of the world and, when I least expected it, love was reborn in me. Back in Buenos Aires, I met Kieran, my loving Irish husband, and we got married in July 2019, with God as our mainstay.

It was time for me to give back as much as I had received. Instead, life rewarded me with genuine love. Unspeakable love. This is how I left behind my structured life in the financial system and jumped into my beautiful project called Sentirse Amada.

For all of the above, I know I can help you. Learn more by joining my community. Let's keep walking together at www.sentirseamada.com[1].

---

1.   http://www.sentirseamada.com/

How do you sleep at night?

We can all agree that it is impossible to fix something we do not know is broken, right? Similarly, we cannot fix our sleeping problems unless we identify what is not right within us.

Therefore, before venturing into the concept of *heart cleansing*, we must take a few moments to think about the *causes of sleep disruption*.

I have been holding workshops to assist people with sleeping problems for some time now, and I have observed some *recurring behaviors*.

When someone signs up for my workshop, I ask her about the quality of her rest. Some people begin by saying, *'It is not very regular, sometimes it's hard to fall asleep, and I wake up at 3 am.'* Others open up and confess, *'It's bad, I wake up several times, and it's almost impossible to fall back asleep.'* But most people just say a few words, like *'disrupted'* or *'insomnia.'*

Afterward, I ask them to tell me if they have any specific problem before falling asleep and how they cope with it.

Some people state that they aren't worried and just fall asleep with no problems. Others talk about anxiety, sorrow, pills, stress, insomnia, issue-related tension, thoughts, noise, fear, or sadness. Here are some of the answers I usually get:

- *'My head keeps spinning, and I worry about everything.'*

- *'When I close my eyes, I get dizzy, I feel I'm going backward very fast, I try to breathe to get a hold of myself.'*

- *'I feel scared of not being able to sleep.'*

I go on to ask them what they wish to change or improve about their current sleeping habits. Do you relate to any of the below?

I wish I could sleep and wake up feeling rested.

I would like to sleep soundly and truly relax my mind.

I wish my sleep was pleasant and relaxing.

I wish I could sleep the whole night through.

I want to shut down my mind and just rest.

Once I know my students' feelings and goals, I ask them about their daily activities and how they take care of themselves. I usually hear answers like:

I go for a walk every day.

I meditate and connect to the here and now.

I pray frequently.

I use relaxation techniques and sleep half an hour during the day.

I read.

I drink tea.

I keep a healthy diet.

I get a massage and practice yoga.

I listen to relaxing music.

All these activities are helpful to accompany the process and techniques that we will review in the following pages, *so we will come back to them later on.*

However, there are some students who, despite repeating these routines for their well-being, are unable to achieve a good night's rest. What is the problem? Let's take a look.

Do you know why you wake up at night?

Each hour you wake up unintentionally has a significance that is related to your organs and emotions.(1) According to traditional Chinese medicine, a poor sleep cycle can reveal many details about your physical and emotional state.

Therefore, it is vital to listen to what your body is telling you and when.

9:00 pm - 11:00 pm

Having trouble falling asleep between 9:00 pm and 11:00 pm could be a sign of stress. Try to relax half an hour before your sleeping time. Avoid noise and lights from your phone, tablet, or television. If possible, practice meditation or centering prayer. Later we will see some recommendations to reduce the symptoms of stress.

11:00 pm - 1:00 am

Waking up between 11:00 pm and 1:00 am could signify emotional disappointment. At this time, the gallbladder is active. It's a perfect moment to practices mantras. Forgive and accept yourself as you are, a unique being worthy of love.

1:00 am - 3:00 am

Waking up between 1:00 am and 3:00 am is related to the accumulation of anger. This meridian connects to the liver and is associated with rage and excess of Yang energy. Have a glass of cold water and meditate for a moment on the source of your distress. Are you able to do something about it? Or would it be better to let go? Decompress your chest and liver area with several breaths focused on the place in your body that resonates with you at that moment.

3:00 am - 5:00 am

If you wake up between 3:00 am and 5:00 am, it may be due to something trying to communicate with you. This hour is related to sadness and the lungs. Pray and do breathing exercises to get back to sleep. I will share with you a meditation to ward off sadness in just a few chapters.

5:00 am - 7:00 am

If you wake up between 5:00 am, and 7:00 am, you might be experiencing an emotional block. The intestine's energy is active at this time, and it means that you have repressed emotions.

Stretch your muscles and try to go to the toilet. They say that our digestive system is our second brain. That is why you must connect your thoughts with your intestines, passing through your heart.

A good tip is to write the first thing that comes to your mind on a piece of paper (keep it handy on your nightstand), and don't stop to think about how you do it. This will help you identify the situations that are affecting you without your knowing it. The more you know about yourself, the easier it will be to detect your emotions and choose how they affect you.

Feelings are neither good nor bad. They are simply part of your humanity. By reviewing situations that cause you emotional pain, resistance, or stomach pain, you can identify the source of your discomfort and begin to feel better.

It is part of the healing process. Keep a positive attitude; everything shall pass!

Later on, I will help you recognize your emotions with an efficient list that will allow you to put them into words—the first step towards inner liberation.

Some studies show that human beings have become accustomed to a phenomenon called *interrupted sleep*. That is, we sleep for four hours, wake up for one or two, and then sleep another four. We have learned to ignore our biological clock!

Ideally, you should use the insomnia hours to meditate, write, drink some tea, or simply relax until you can sleep again. During this time, your brain produces prolactin, which is a hormone that promotes relaxation.

It's essential to consider your body's subtle physical, emotional, and spiritual signals and value them accordingly. Learning to listen and understand what your body is telling you is crucial to know yourself.

Reflect upon the following questions:

What do you want?

What do you wish to radiate?

Do you want to self-transcend?

These questions invite you to live more consciously and intensely. *You do yourself no favors by going to sleep with negative thoughts.* You will carry the nightmares around with you all throughout the next day, monks say.

I want to share with you a passage from one of my favorite books, *Man's Search for Meaning*. Here Viktor Frankl explains anticipatory anxiety (pages 152-155):

The paradoxical intention also applies in cases of sleep disorder. The fear of insomnia produces a hyper-intention to fall asleep that, in turn, prevents the patient from achieving it. To overcome this fear, I advise the patient to resist sleeping, to stay awake. In other words, the hyper-intention to fall asleep, born of anticipatory anxiety of not succeeding, must be replaced by the paradoxical intention of not to fall asleep, which will surely soon be followed by sleep. The paradoxical intention ... constitutes a strategy of short-term effects ... The key to healing is found in self-transcendence, in the transcendence of oneself.

How Sleep Affects IQ

Tel Aviv University expert Avi Sadeh found that poor sleep affects intelligence and reduces impulse control.

You probably didn't think that an hour less sleep meant a decrease in your IQ. However, Avi Sadeh noted that: *'The loss of one hour of sleep is equivalent to the loss of two years of cognitive maturation and development.'(2)*

Loss of sleep weakens our ability to coordinate thoughts to achieve a goal and perceive the consequences of actions.

This is why tired people also have difficulty controlling their impulses. A tired brain gets "stuck" on incorrect answers and cannot develop creative solutions to our problems.

When we are tired, it is actually more challenging to be happy because we recall negative memories more than positive ones.

Many daily activities affect our IQ without our knowing it. And the disruption of the sleep pattern is one of the main ones. (3)

According to the American Psychological Association, sleep is essential for a person's health and well-being. However, millions of people do not get enough sleep or suffer from lack of sleep.

Surveys conducted by the National Science Foundation (NSF) between 1999 and 2004 reveal that at least 40 million Americans suffer from *more than 70 different sleep disorders*, and 60% of adults report having *problems sleeping a few nights a week or more.* Most people with these problems go undiagnosed and untreated.

In the August 2004 issue of *Sleep* magazine, Dr. Timothy Roehrs, director of research at the Center for Sleep Disorders and Research at Henry Ford Hospital in Detroit, published one of the first studies to measure *the effects of sleepiness on decision-making and risk-taking.*

Dr. Roehrs and his colleagues gave sleepy and alert individuals prompt to complete a series of computer tasks. At random times, they were given the option *to take their money and stop or move on with the risk of losing everything* if they didn't complete their work in a specified amount of time. The researchers found that alert individuals were susceptible to the amount of work they needed to finish tasks and *understood the risk of losing their money.* Instead, sleepy subjects chose *to abandon the tasks prematurely or risked losing everything*, even when it was unlikely that they would get it done.

Ringing in the Ears

Another effect from lack of sleep that many people experience is a *ringing in the ears*, which can also be described as roaring, hissing, humming, or buzzing. The noise usually lasts only a few minutes. But when it doesn't improve or go away, it's called *tinnitus.*

Tinnitus is exhausting, and its origin can be found in emotional distress.

I experienced it myself during very stressful episodes throughout my life—when I had to take an exam, changed jobs, got married, or moved.

What helped me calm my symptoms until they disappeared utterly was *centering meditation or contemplative prayer*, accompanied by heart cleansing.

If you also suffer from discomfort, you must find out the causes and put them into words. This is the only way that annoying buzzing will start to go away. I am sure of it.

How can you discover the origin? By keeping a journal of what affects you. As a title for each day, write down how intense the sound was: <u>loud, medium, or soft</u>. You will little by little discover any relationship between the intensity of the sound and the events you experienced each day.

If you don't know where to start, I invite you to answer these self-examination questions to find out *where your stress or worry is coming from.*

<u>Exercises:</u>

What daily activity overwhelms you the most? Go over what happened yesterday and ask yourself:

What worried you the most?

In what part of your body did you feel it?

Did you ever feel this way when you were younger?

Was there something you heard and "didn't want to hear"? Was there something that was negatively told to you?

I understand what you are going through. Both insomnia and tinnitus are consequences of something more profound. But these questions will help you look into your deepest feelings. Which, these days, is no easy task.

Nap or no nap, that is the question

In my experience, the answer to whether we should sleep during the day is *a resounding yes*. The siesta is a sacred moment. I come from a swelteringly hot area, and napping is more than a good habit. *It is a fundamental necessity.*

Sleep research proves that taking a nap of up to 20 minutes, between 1 and 4 pm, is ideal to continue the rest of the day *full of energy*. It also makes it possible to be more attentive and continue work activity with enthusiasm.

According to Daniel Vigo, a medical researcher at the National Council for Scientific and Technical Research (CONICET) of Argentina and professor at the Argentine Catholic University, *a person's alertness biologically decreases between 1 and 3 pm.*

For this reason, a nap of up to 20 minutes is beneficial since it improves alertness, attention and mood. If a person sleeps about 8 hours at night, a 20-minute nap before 4 pm will be enough.

We call this a *power nap*. It is short enough to avoid falling into a deep sleep and allows us to continue working with great enthusiasm.(4) This duration prevents inertia sleep, i.e., a feeling of lightheadedness experienced when waking up after more than an hour.

Sleep hygiene or heart cleansing

♥ *This is a simple way to sustain our decision to love throughout the day.* ♥

Sleeping for a certain number of hours is not enough to guarantee that you will sleep restfully. To wake up with renewed energy to live each day to the fullest, you need quality sleep.

For this reason, going to bed with a clean heart, free of pressure, anguish, and stress, is fundamental.

What is sleep hygiene or heart cleansing?

After a long day, your body needs a comforting bath to recover from the traces of your daily tasks. *But what about your heart?*

Your heart also stores all the experiences lived throughout the day ... and it needs a hygiene ritual to go to sleep peacefully!

You probably have nights when sleeping becomes challenging and distressing. You feel uneasy, as if something were pressing on your chest. You toss, you turn. Your thoughts flit through your head like an endless whirlwind.

According to Inés Ordoñez de Lanús, the founder of the Santa María Ordoñez spirituality center, *serenity and peace at bedtime are vital. And for this, the heart cleansing ritual can help enormously.* (5)

Heart hygiene consists of small wellness practices to carry out an internal analysis of how your day went, observing each situation, thinking about who you met, and how you felt.

It is an experiential technique that will require your commitment to answer and reflect upon different questions. With practice, you will be able to release tension and cleanse your heart and mind to get a good night's sleep.

Before continuing with the reading, I recommend keeping something to take notes with: a personal notebook, diary, or simply the notes application on your phone. If you are reading the print version of this book, you can also write in the blank spaces I left for that purpose.

Daily prayer will help you get to know yourself better, understand who you really are in your purest state, and be more present in the now. This means being more aware of each situation that you have to live through.

Examples of NOT being aware are:

thinking about the next activity, the next thing on your agenda

not enjoying what you are doing at this moment

not listening to whoever is in front of you with your full attention.

Listening while being present is *an act of love.*

Your presence, not only physical but also of mind and spirit, will allow you to bring to prayer all your experiences (feelings, perceptions, sensations). It will help you to cleanse your heart thoroughly at the end of the day.

Exercise:

Take three deep breaths and ask yourself: How do I feel about what I have just read? Try to identify and name at least <u>three emotions</u>: Write them down because we will come back to them later on:

1-

2-

3-

What <u>thoughts</u> came to your mind before sleeping?

1-

2-

3-

Go over your day and think about every situation you've been involved in:

Who did you meet?

How did they look at you? Was it with love or contempt?

Did you listen to yourself?

Did you enjoy the encounter, or was your mind thinking about what you had to do next?

✍ Take your notepad and let your hand write freely. Do not stop. Let it flow and write down whatever you feel within you.

I invite you to share your experience in the book's comments or on my website. I would love to hear which tips or recommendations enriched you the most or worked best for you. You will be amazed at what you have to offer!

To learn more on meditation or contemplative, centering silent prayer, download my e-book Learn to Pray in 20 Minutes: Contemplative Prayer as a Source of Life. *You can find it at www.sentirseamada.com/regalo or on Amazon for the print edition.*

Heart hygiene: two practical exercises

♥♥ "The beauty of things exists in the spirit of those who contemplate them." (D. Hume)♥♥

There are two fundamental rituals you can perform at the end of the day to cleanse your heart:

The daily assessment

The discernment process

Daily assessment

Start with a sign. In my case, I make the sign of the Cross and repeat the Our Father prayer. I love stopping at each word and meditating on what resonates with me (if it comes out quickly from memory, that's also okay).

I know that while praying, I am in the presence of the Lord, creator of all of nature, source of love and energy.

I ask *Him* to help to:

Go over my day, from the moment I woke up to this very moment.

Help me review every situation I was involved in, my work, my journey, everything I did, and the places I visited.

Remember every person I came across throughout the day and visualize each of their faces.

I let my breath run through my body, and I think about how it felt when waking up. I become aware that this new day is a gift from life. I take deep breaths many times.

To achieve heart hygiene, you must go through five phases, each one dedicated to a different aspect of your being: your mind, your body, your actions, the people in your life, your forgiveness.

The Mental Phase

To start, ask yourself about your thoughts throughout the day. What was your first thought that morning when you opened your eyes? What came to your mind? The day's schedule, the first meeting? What was your first feeling about the new day? Reluctance, displeasure, guilt, gratitude?

To help you retain your reflections, you can make a list of what you usually feel when you wake up:

The Body Phase

Focus on the physical aspect of your day. How did your body feel when you woke up? Did your neck, back, or waist hurt? Did you rest well? Did you stretch with pleasure, or were you tense all day? Did you hug someone when you woke up, or did you want to? Why?

Open your arms and remain with your eyes closed. Imagine the enormous grace that life gives you tonight: you are doing something precious, unique. Your hands help, your gaze helps, your body helps. Thank them.

Take another deep breath and keep thinking about each of the places you visited. How did you feel in them: at ease, uncomfortable, attacked, received, happy, upset? Did you want to enter, or were you forced to go, to comply, to look good, because you didn't know how to say no? Could you BE yourself everywhere? Or did you have to play a role according to what was expected of you? What was your attitude in these places? Did you feel positive or not so much?

The Action Phase

Now is the time to think about your acts and actions. Take a deep breath and remember everything you did—your tasks, your jobs, your activities.

What was your contribution today? Did you do or say something that you regret or for which you have to apologize? How was your inner attitude while going through your routine? Did you enjoy it, or did you do it, again, out of obligation? What thoughts, words, gestures, sensations, and emotions accompanied you at work or at home? What was the most beautiful thing you did, what did you like or enjoy the most?

What was it you did very well? Did it go the way you wanted? Was there something you did wrong or that you didn't do out of laziness? What could you have done with more love and dedication?

The People Phase

Breathe deeply. Remember each of the people you met throughout the day and who you helped, accompanied, assisted, or could not help.

Try to realize the emotions you experienced in each encounter and try to express them positively or negatively.

What was the most beautiful and joyful thing that you experienced in your encounters with others? What was the most joyous thing about that meeting? What still resonates in your heart at the end of this day? What was the most demanding meeting for you? Who was it difficult for you to be with or talk to?

In what ways did each person you meet help you grow in your own identity as a woman? Did they make you feel present to yourself, to others, and to everything you lived? How did your emotions translate into concrete acts and gestures of love?

Relive your emotions and express your heart to the Lord. Don't be afraid to speak what you felt and perhaps did not know or could not put down in words.

The Forgiveness Phase

We have reached the last phase. Breathe deeply. Become aware of your thoughts, words, emotions, bodily sensations, and actions by confronting them with the light of LOVE.

What situations made you impatient, angered you, got you out of character? What impacted your heart most strongly? Was there something you did or said that you regret or that you need to apologize for? What could you have done with more love and dedication? Is there someone you have to forgive?

Take another deep breath. How is your heart at the end of this day? What do you want to say to God? What do you need to thank Him for?

Take a deep breath and focus on how you feel right now. Try to identify and name your feelings.

Put your hands on your heart, as if wanting to "touch" what you feel, caress the experience lived throughout the day.

You can make a wish or an intention for the people you have seen. Remember, if you can, their faces and wish them well. If you can't remember their faces or pinpoint their names, simply give a blessing and a good wish for all of them.

Thank life for having been with these people today. Open your arms as if wanting to let go of this experience, give it to life... Wish everyone well and let them go ...

Take a few deep breaths, and as the air moves in and out of your body, repeat:

This was my day ...

I did my best...

That's how it went...

Breathe deeply. Become aware of your interiority. Stay like this for a few minutes, considering the day that passed with love.

Trust in the maternal arms of Mary. Pray Hail Mary, make the sign of the Cross, and get ready to sleep in peace.

Let your heart glow. Keep repeating, to the beat of your heart, the name of the Lord or your favorite phrase to relax. If you are of another spiritual orientation, you can repeat your favorite mantra.

Record every moment of your day

To live an authentic experience of God in my life every night and to achieve spiritual harmony, I use some tools. This table helps organize my evaluation or review for the day.

I share it with you in the hopes that it will help you take the first steps. I hope you enjoy completing it and find that what you discover is enriching for you:

Daily assessment

Date:

1- Name that summarizes or identifies the day:

2- Internal review of experiences:

Spiritual state that prevailed:

Description:

3- Main experiences:

What happened to me? In what circumstances? Where do these feelings come from? Where do they take me? How do I respond? Positively? Who do I share with? How to overcome the rejection reaction?

4- Discernment for the moment

5- Message of the day:

6- The task that springs or arises from the feeling of the day:

"I want to give myself to God, let go and not be stubborn about something that hurts me and ties me to the past. By letting go, I open myself to the beautiful mystery of life, the insecurities of what is to come, and the challenges of what I don't know."

"Without resignation, there would be no butterfly."

7- Acknowledgments.

After completing the table, ask yourself:

What difficulties did I find in completing it or will arise when experiencing my nocturnal reflection?

What process can help me in my growth and spiritual integration?

What traces of my history do I see in the dynamics of these exercises for finding the source?

Believe in that spring, the Living Water, God, who comes to your aid. Because where the water can go in, there is healing.

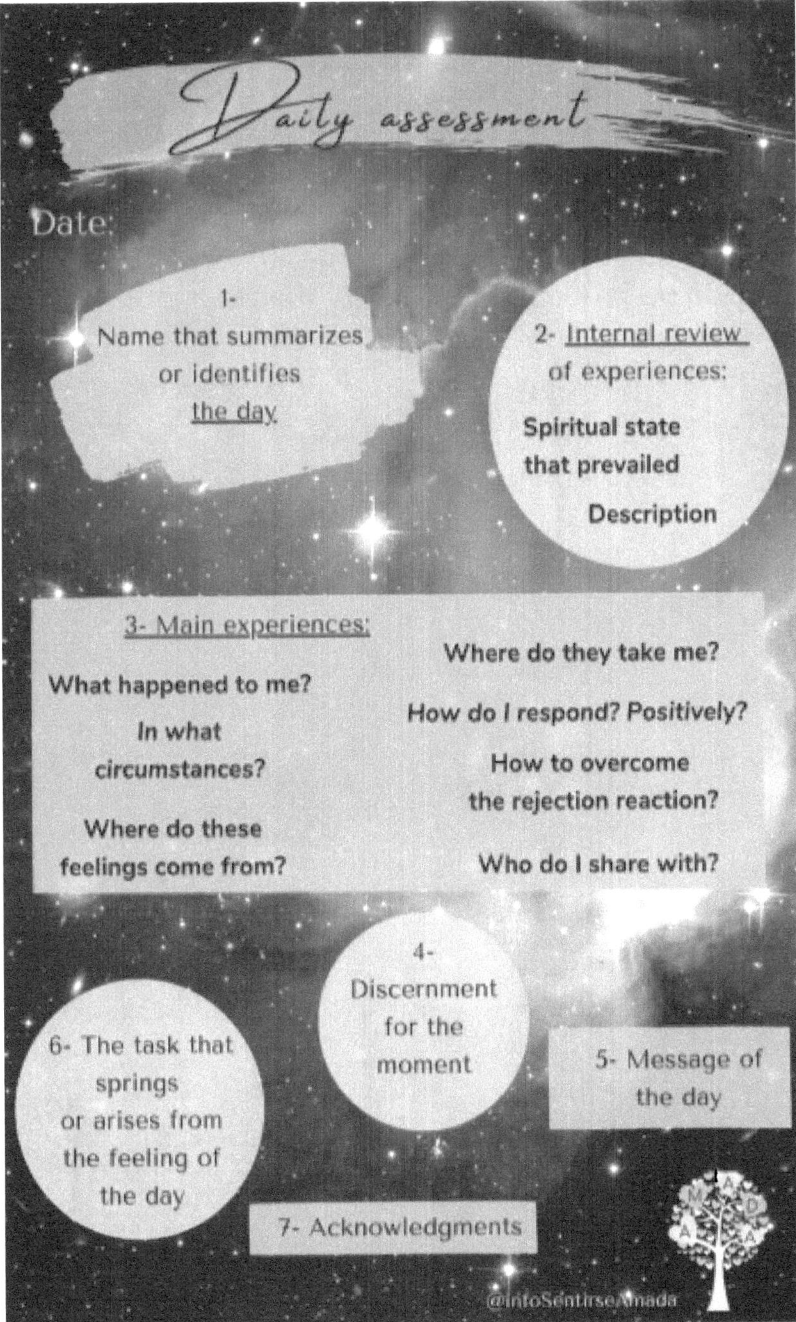
Daily assessment
Date:
1-
Name that summarizes
or identifies
the day
2- Internal review
of experiences:
Spiritual state
that prevailed
Description
3- Main experiences:
What happened to me?
In what
circumstances?
Where do these
feelings come from?
Where do they take me?
How do I respond? Positively?
How to overcome
the rejection reaction?
Who do I share with?
4-
Discernment
for the
moment
6- The task that
springs
or arises from
the feeling of
the day
5- Message of
the day
7- Acknowledgments
@InfoSentirseAmada

The Discernment Process

After repeating the practice of heart cleansing or hygiene many times, you will become more experienced in the discernment process.

The discernment process is a form of grace to recognize God in every moment of your day and, more importantly, connect His desires with yours. It involves adopting a refreshing attitude. A challenging but not impossible task, believe me.

The discernment process consists of seven simple but highly effective steps that you can apply daily:

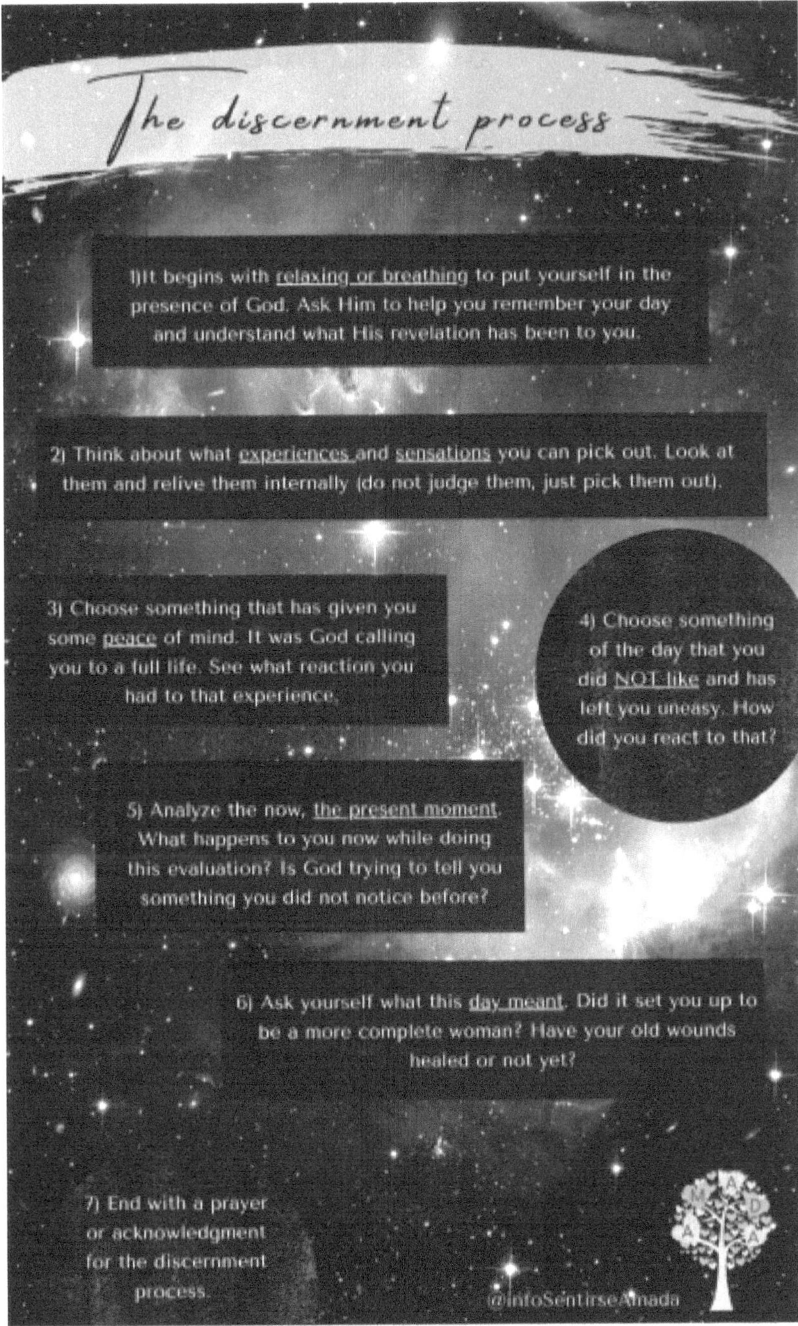

The discernment process

1) It begins with relaxing or breathing to put yourself in the presence of God. Ask Him to help you remember your day and understand what His revelation has been to you.

2) Think about what experiences and sensations you can pick out. Look at them and relive them internally (do not judge them, just pick them out).

3) Choose something that has given you some peace of mind. It was God calling you to a full life. See what reaction you had to that experience.

4) Choose something of the day that you did NOT like and has left you uneasy. How did you react to that?

5) Analyze the now, the present moment. What happens to you now while doing this evaluation? Is God trying to tell you something you did not notice before?

6) Ask yourself what this day meant. Did it set you up to be a more complete woman? Have your old wounds healed or not yet?

7) End with a prayer or acknowledgment for the discernment process.

@infoSentirseAmada

Begin to heal

"Your life is too precious to ruin because of resentment."

Many people do not get a good night's sleep because bitterness has made a nest in their hearts. They get up angry and moody and often don't even know the reason for their discomfort.

One of the main causes of negative feelings is the oppressive thoughts that stir in the mind during sleep, resulting from a lack of forgiveness.

The pressure you endure affects your body, causing anxiety and nervousness every morning.

God created us to live in harmony and to be in a delicate balance. *Your life is too precious to ruin because of resentment.*

Some women cannot forgive or accept themselves or others. They may even be so angry at God that they fail to realize that they need to forgive.

Recognizing emotions and honoring them is the first step to healing.

Recognize and honor your emotions

Before beginning my process of reconnecting with God, it was difficult for me to understand what I was feeling. But acknowledging the emotions in me was the first step to learning to recognize myself as more human, more imperfect, and much more lovable.

Being aware of what you feel is important to better understand your actions and your body's reactions.

For example, if you are impulsive, you can early recognize the first symptoms of stress in your body and prevent them from turning into something more serious. Realize what actions you find exciting and spend your time doing more of what is good for you and less of what exhausts you.

I want to share with you two lists: one with positive emotions and the other with negative emotions. They will help you put a name to your feelings and honor them.

I propose that you make a mark next to each emotion you <u>perceived today</u>. Stop at each one and ask yourself when you felt it, where it affected you, how it made you feel, what your inner voice told you.

This exercise is invaluable in getting to know the real you. Still, you must be honest with yourself and consider your actions and character traits *even if you do not like them*. In the long run, a greater awareness of yourself will benefit you greatly.

From the heart, I hope you find it helpful.

Positive emotions

Admiration

Affection

Amusement

Bravery

Calm

Carefulness

Closeness

Comfort

Commitment

Compassion

Confidence

Connection

Conviction

Courage

Curiosity

Delight

Eagerness

Ease

Elation

Emotion

Empathy
Enjoyment
Enthusiasm
Euphoria
Excitement
Expectation
Fascination
Fondness
Fortune
Freedom
Fulfillment
Generosity
Gratitude
Happiness
Hope
Independence
Inspiration
Interest
Intrigue
Joy
Jubilation
Love
Mercy
Modesty
Motivation
Nostalgia
Openness
Optimism
Passion
Peace
Piety
Preparation

Pride
Prosperity
Prudence
Relaxation
Relief
Renovation
Satisfaction
Self-confidence
Serenity
Solidarity
Strength
Superiority
Surprise
Tenderness
Tranquility
Unity
Victory
Vitality
Wonder

Negative emotions
Abandonment
Loathing
Alarm
Anger
Anguish
Annoyance
Anxiety
Apathy
Aversion
Bewilderment

Bitterness
Boredom
Burden
Concern
Confusion
Cowardice
Demotivation
Depression
Despair
Despondency
Disappointment
Discomfort
Dejection
Discontent
Discouragement
Disenchantment
Disgust
Disillusionment
Dislike
Dissatisfaction
Distrust
Envy
Exasperation
Exhaustion
Fatigue
Fear
Panic
Frustration
Fury
Futility
Grief
Grudge

Grumpiness
Guilt
Hate
Hopelessness
Horror
Hostility
Impatience
Powerlessness
Inability
Indecision
Indifference
Indignation
Inferiority
Instability
Irritation
Isolation
Jealousy
Laziness
Lethargy
Loneliness
Mediocrity
Melancholia
Misery
Misfortune
Nervousness
Nuisance
Pain
Paralysis
Pessimism
Pride
Rage
Repentance

Repulsion
Resentment
Restlessness
Antagonism
Sadness
Dread
Shame
Shock
Skepticism
Sorrow
Weakness
Suspicion
Tension
Terror
Tiredness
Unhappiness
Danger
Violence
Weariness
Worry

How to get rid of resentment

If you took alternate paths to faith, chances are you were not able to deal with resentment or you struggled. You didn't know that the solution is in God and in His grace.

If you stray from His path, *you will only add new bitterness to your spirit* and a feeling of loneliness and helplessness.

But you must not blame others. Even if someone else has been responsible for your suffering, *you have the responsibility to decide what to do with your own resentment.*

After you've gone through every last corner of your heart, you may realize you need to forgive or ask forgiveness for something you did unintentionally. In this way, *you will be able to eliminate any trace of resentment* in your heart.

But what if the person we must forgive is no longer close to us and we cannot talk to them? If forgiveness is deep, reconciliation is always possible.

Let me share this exercise to guide you on this path. Repeat these phrases (and, if you want, put soft music on in the background):

Dear God, I,...................., renew my decision to forgive .... for every offense, humiliation, abandonment, resentment, rejection, insult, lie, scam, and lack of appreciation and love.

Take a deep breath and say everything that comes to your mind.

Imagine Jesus sitting next to you and explain to him your pain and bitterness.

Finally, ask him to release you from all resentment by the grace of forgiveness towards ....

By His Divine Heart, I forgive you, ..., I bless you in your health and declare you free. You no longer owe me anything.

I ask God to love you deeply and fill you with His peace. Amen.

If you don't reveal your life's wounds to the light of God, you won't be able to heal the pain in your heart. Through your own defense mechanisms, you'll be mired more deeply in frustration and bitterness every day.

That feeling of non-sense will accompany you along with your own weaknesses.

How many nights do you come home with the sole idea of going to bed, resting, sleeping, and forgetting everything?

It is in those moments that God expects you to come to Him so that, like a gentle night breeze, *He can guide you* toward your life purpose.

Women were dreamed of in love and to love here and now. We must start by *acknowledging our emotions and honoring them.*

To forgive

Dear God, I, ... , renew my decision to forgive .... for every offense, humiliation, abandonment, resentment, rejection, insult, lie, scam, and lack of appreciation and love.

Take a deep breath and say everything that comes to your mind.

Imagine Jesus sitting next to you and explain to him your pain and bitterness.

Finally, ask him to release you from all resentment by the grace of forgiveness towards ....

By His Divine Heart, I forgive you, ..., I bless you in your health and declare you free. You no longer owe me anything.

I ask God to love you deeply and fill you with His peace.
Amen.

Distance healing

God is close to us in every moment of our journey. Therefore, He can heal us and heal the fractures that fragment us internally *if we make room for Him in our lives and our hearts.*

Just ask Him: "*God, make rivers of living water run in my heart, quench the thirst for love, peace, and happiness that is in me.*"

Have faith that everything will pass. This will also pass, '*because you, my Lord, are my help*' (Psalm 63:8). Imagine Jesus using scissors to cut the ties of resentment that bind you to someone.

This ritual also applies when you ask for the healing of another person. If you pray with trust in God, *you can ask Him to bless that person* from a distance and touch their lives with His love.

♥♥ *"Looking for the good of our fellows we find ours." (Plato)* ♥♥

Remember that the most important thing is determination:

Forgiveness begins when you decide to forgive.

Pray for the person who hurt you. Bless her or him.

As much as possible, talk to the person, clarify the situation. If it is not possible, leave everything in the hands of God through prayer. (Gustavo Jamut)

Exercise:

Push the wall.

Step 1: Stand up facing the wall.

Step 2: Rest your hands on the wall.

Step 3: Push the wall with all your strength.

Step 4: Keep pushing the wall.

Step 5: Put your hands on your heart, as if wanting to "touch" what you feel, caress the lived experience of pushing the wall and reflect: Did the wall move? What did you feel when you made it? How did your body feel? Which parts of your body?

Final step: Think of the wall as your life: What aspects of your life do you want to push away? Choose a word that represents your feelings and write it down here: ....

Ten tips for better sleep

We have seen that optimizing your night's rest is essential to maintaining 100 percent mental acuity. It also contributes to achieving an emotional balance and a maximum energy level throughout the day. But how do we reach optimal rest?

Here are ten clear and actionable tips that you can put into practice today to leverage everything we have learned in the previous chapters. (6)

1- Take care of your environment

Create a suitable environment to rest where you feel comfortable and nothing interrupts your sleep.

Some people prefer total silence. Others feel better with white noise, such as a song on repeat or the sound of a fan.

It is also essential that you be relaxed at bedtime. If you've just done something exciting, it's a good idea to wait a bit before going to bed. You can also apply relaxation techniques to calm and free yourself from daily stress (this is an excellent time to practice heart cleansing).

2- Follow a ritual and establish a bedtime schedule

The more consistent you are with the time you wake up, the more regular your bodily functions will be. The National Sleep Foundation of America recommends having a bedtime and wake-up time and sticking to them as much as possible.

It is not about having a strict schedule but helping your body get used to a routine that allows you to sleep the necessary hours. Do not go to bed late at night if you start work early.

3- Take care of your diet

Food can influence your sleep. The quality of your food and the time of day you eat can affect your general well-being and become a problem at bedtime.

Ideally, dinner should be light, although it is not good to go to sleep hungry because you risk waking up during the night. Also, be sure not to eat anything that causes heartburn, as the symptoms can be pretty unpleasant.

Although *alcohol* can make you drowsy, it does not allow quality rest since it causes fragmented sleep. You will fall asleep faster due to its depressing effect, but your sleep phases will be affected, and you will not get the rest you need.

4- Avoid stimulants after mid-afternoon

Coffee is healthy if consumed in moderation as it stimulates the brain. However, when it is drunk in large quantities, it can interfere with sleep and even cause tremors, nervousness, and an irregular pulse.

Now, coffee is so embedded in our culture that it is hard to avoid it entirely.

If you do not want to stop consuming coffee, a good option is to *drink it only in the mornings* and say *no* after mid-afternoon. The same applies for tea, mate, or cola sodas.

5- Practice physical exercise

Exercising regularly helps people sleep better. However, its benefits depend on the time of the day you do the activity and your general physical condition.

Some experts say that exercising in the morning does not affect your night's sleep and even helps improve it. In contrast, *exercising very close to bedtime, especially at high intensity, can cause sleep disturbances.*

After an intense training session, it can take up to four hours for the body to fully recover and return to a state that allows for proper rest.

6- Do not oversleep at naptime

Napping has positive effects on well-being and can increase or improve alertness, concentration, productivity, memory, and learning ability.

But to avoid nap affecting sleep patterns during the night, it is preferable that it does not last more than 20 or 30 minutes and that it is not too late in the day.

7- If you can't get to sleep, get up

At any time, if you can't fall asleep, get up and do an activity that induces you to sleep—perform a relaxation technique, read a book. Taking a hot shower is also effective as raising your temperature and then lowering it causes your body to produce melatonin. This hormone plays a key role in regulating the sleep-wake cycle.

It is better not to stay in bed, but don't overdo it. Either of these things can increase your anxiety level.

8- Clear your head

Stress, worries, or anger about something that happened during the day can creep into your mind just before you go to sleep and disrupt your rest.

Therefore, if you suffer from anxiety or are going through a hard time, you must learn to control your thoughts (*heart hygiene*). Incorporating a routine of meditation or progressive relaxation before going to sleep can be a good idea.

If your anxiety level is high, take a few moments throughout the day (not just before bedtime) to get some alone time and do breathing exercises.

9- Establish a curfew for electronic devices

Stick to a strict time limit on the use of electronic devices. Try not to check your social networks or email and avoid watching television *at least ninety minutes before your bedtime.*

It may be tempting to watch marathons of your favorite shows, but prioritizing your sleep is more important.

If your daily routine does not allow you to do without your devices an hour and a half before sleeping, *start with just fifteen minutes and increase the time each day.* You will see how much your rest improves.

10- Staying informed is important, but not just before bed

Limit the type of media you consume. In particular, try not to watch shows that increase your anxiety in the afternoon.

This is perhaps the most difficult advice to follow, but also the most sensible. Watch the news only once a day and, if possible, do so in the morning.

A few minutes a night to shine the next day

There is a simple but effective routine to achieve success every day.

<u>Start at the end</u>

At the end of the day, take your schedule and open it to the next day's page. (7) Make a list of everything you have to do. Writing what you should do the night before means *you can prepare for it while you are sleeping.*

In the list you can write everything, from the smallest to the largest:

Cook my own breakfast (not grab something to go)

Take my medicine

Get 15 minutes of exercise

Pay the bills

The goal is for you to write down the simplest things that *you think you can do* but that you often leave out because you think, "I'll do it later."

<u>Make a decision</u>

Think about the most essential things that can change your life if you repeat them every day. Before sleeping, you have to fight the following battles:

Will you eat nutritious meals, or will you keep gravitating towards unhealthy food?

Will you exercise more or sleep more than you need?

Will you grow intellectually, or will you waste time on social media?

Will you improve your relationship with others, or will you distance yourself from them?

These answers can lead you down different paths. Of course, you don't always have to be an ideal person. Everyone has days when they can afford to do whatever they want. But the goal is that, through these questions, *you plan a truly productive day in which work, well-being, and personal relationships can change for the better.*

Write down the plans, goals, and even the most straightforward actions. The next day, check off each item on your list as you go through it. *You will have a clear vision of everything you have achieved.* Repeat this routine over and over until your nighttime habit is no longer needed to transform your life.

The importance of falling asleep and resting in times of pandemic

Sleeping well is essential to protect you from infection and for your body to react optimally. *But in times of high anxiety, such as a pandemic, falling asleep becomes even more difficult.*

That is why *sleep hygiene* is particularly relevant. This practice helps you not only to sleep more but also to sleep better. (8)

What to do when you feel sick?

If you are fighting an infection, your body needs more rest to heal quickly. (9)

For starters, get two hours more sleep than usual. You can improve your sleeping conditions by *using a wedge-shaped pillow or additional pillows to keep your chest elevated and prevent further congestion.*

Change your clothes and sheets frequently to control the spread of bacteria or viruses. How nice it is to sleep with clean-smelling sheets!

Prayers for cleansing your heart

Poem to feel peaceful

I sincerely hope that these lines accompany you every night and that you can fall into the restful sleep you deserve. *Your world deserves to receive the gifts you have!*

This wise poem provides excellent fodder for contemplation.

Says the old soul healer:
Don't hurt the back, but the load.
Don't hurt the eyes, but the injustice.
Don't hurt the head, but the thoughts.
Don't hurt the throat, but what is expressed with anger.
Don't hurt the stomach, but what is not digested.
Don't hurt the liver, but the rage.
Doesn't hurt the heart, but the love.
And it's the love itself
That contains THE MOST POWERFUL MEDICINE.

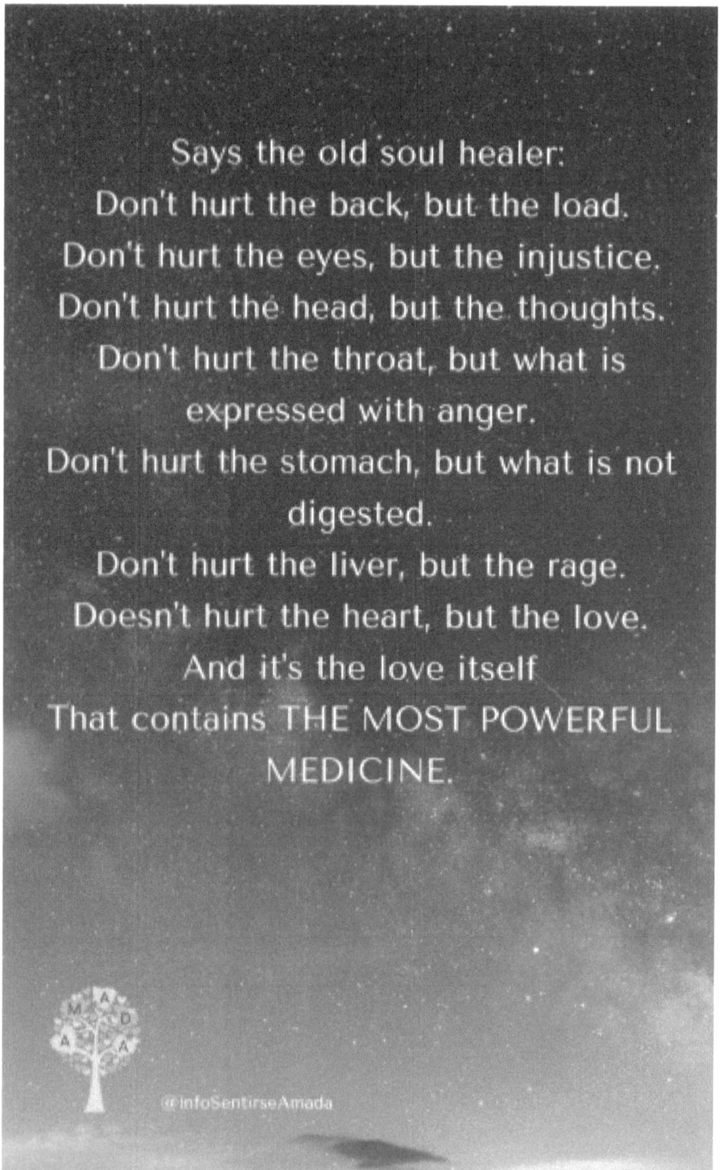

"It doesn't matter what you see in your life today. Everything can be different tomorrow. The darkest night gives way to the brightest morning. Everything will pass. This will also pass, as every storm does. Trust the process and the power you have within you." (Karen Berg)

Ask God for help, and He, *with His immense love*, will comfort you, and you will be able to change anything.

Prayer against distress

This prayer or meditation will help you overcome those moments when you see no way out and seek urgent solace.

Prayer against distress

Dear God, mystery and creator of nature,

You are sensitive,

and know my anguish.

Teach me how to place my fear and powerlessness in You.

Hold me tonight,

So I can be calm and feel closer to You.

In your arms, I feel protected,

And if fear persists, I feel it less heavily.

May my distress get me closer to You, my Lord.

May I feel You next to me as you touch my heart,

I know I will be protected and safe.

I only want to fall asleep in Your arms,

like Your beloved and favorite daughter.

I need to rest for a few hours,

find peace and calm.

I want to place my fear in Your hands,

And that You take them far, far away.

I love You.

AMEN.

Prayer against distress

Dear God, mystery and creator of nature,
You are sensitive,
and know my anguish.
Teach me how to place my fear and
powerlessness in You.
Hold me tonight,
So I can be calm and feel closer to You.
In your arms, I feel protected,
And if fear persists, I feel it less heavily.
May my distress get me closer to You, my Lord.
May I feel You next to me as you touch my heart,
I know I will be protected and safe.
I only want to fall asleep in Your arms,
like Your beloved and favorite daughter.
I need to rest for a few hours,
find peace and calm.
I want to place my fear in Your hands,
And that You take them far, far away.
I love You.
AMEN.

Prayer against sadness

When sadness arises, we need to pull it out somehow so it does not settle in our body or any other part of our body. If we set it free, sadness will happily go away. An excellent way to do this is through this prayer or meditation:

Prayer against sadness

My beloved God,
Tonight, sadness takes hold of my heart
And my whole being and feelings.
I cannot push the sorrow away by myself,
It wells up from deep within my soul,
It shall not let me go on.
I want to place my saddened heart in You
To be filled with your infinite energy.
May You transform my sadness with Your light
So that I embrace You and feel Your love.
And that it be enough for me,
That it be everything.
And that I recognize Your kindness in my sadness,
Because thanks to it, I come to You,
As my only source of true comfort.
And pierced by Your love,
Recover the happiness that transforms my life
Instead of sorrow, give me peace.
That, for Your love,
Through my feeling of sadness
I can feel again loved by You and me.
AMEN.

Prayer against sadness

My beloved God,
Tonight, sadness takes hold of my heart
And my whole being and feelings.
I cannot push the sorrow away by myself,
It wells up from deep within my soul,
It shall not let me go on.
I want to place my saddened heart in You
To be filled with your infinite energy.
May You transform my sadness with Your light
So that I embrace You and feel Your love,
And that it be enough for me,
That it be everything.
And that I recognize Your kindness in my
sadness,
Because thanks to it, I come to You,
As my only source of true comfort.
And pierced by Your love,
Recover the happiness that transforms my life
Instead of sorrow, give me peace.
That, for Your love,
Through my feeling of sadness
I can feel again loved by You and me.
AMEN.

<u>Exercise:</u>

Now it is your turn. Take these prayers and adapt them to what you are feeling.

The versions of the prayers you see here are adaptations that I made myself in moments of anguish and sadness. They are based on the beautiful prayers offered by the Santa María Spirituality Center on its website. I invite you to visit the website, where you find unbelievably valuable related resources.

Tell me, how do you feel after reading these prayers and poems? Visit my website www.sentirseamada.com[1], or send me an email info@sentirseamada.com. I would love to hear your thoughts!

---

1.   *http://www.sentirseamada.com*

Our encounter is coming to an end

Before saying goodbye, I want to share some thoughts about sleep meditation, the path to encountering God.

Rafael Cabarrús explains in *Cuaderno de Bitácora* (210-212):

Our dreams always communicate a message, and they invite our subconscious to work upon them so they grow, like raw material to pray to God. (10)

Just by working under God, *He* reveals the most intimate secrets of your heart. He heals it and enhances your strengths so you can share them with others.

To analyze your dreams in terms of prayer:

Start by making a request to God. For instance, ask Him to show you who you are, to show you the truth. It could be helpful to have Psalm 139 playing in the background.

Work on the different symbols and topics of the dream (sensation of images, sounds, smells, the context, the plot), and make a new request to the Lord.

Reflect upon the body posture during the dream and ask the Lord to help you heal and rise.

Look into the positive aspects of your dream and ask the Lord to enhance them.

Ask Him to unveil to you what it is like to be better, to rise up, to overcome your own weaknesses, to grow in His company offering your light to others.

I would love for you to join me in my next steps so we can keep walking together and I can share more with you about my passions. Follow me on social media (@infosentirseamada) and visit my website www.sentirseamada.com[1] to get all my latest news.

Blessings. ♥

Yenni

---

1. *http://www.sentirseamada.com*

GLOSSARY

In spiritual accompaniment and coaching, we use many different and specific terms to explain how our body and mind work under stress. In this brief glossary, I included some of the most important such terms for you to check while reading the book. You will also find links to my blog, where you can learn more about these concepts and keep making progress on your spiritual development.

Adaptability: This refers to how flexible our brain and neurons are. It is what allows us to face many stressful situations with resilience, depending on our ability to adapt. If we become more flexible, adapt to stressful situations, and learn to make our way through the pain, we can easily recover. People who do not adapt and do not let themselves change tend to always present the same chronic symptoms over time because they can't get rid of the stressing factor. Why is this? Because they stare at the problem from the outside, not from the inside.

Bodily sensations: These are physiological changes that appear when connecting to a particular event (positive or negative).

Change of perception: This is an accompaniment resource that is used to redefine an experience. It is a tool that is applied in exercises to provide a new vision or perspective. It helps by opening up a healthier and less stressful way of regarding the past. It won't change your history, but it can change how you interpret it. We can change the meaning we attribute to experiences and help our unconscious go through the pain and transform it.

Childhood wounds: These are experiences and situations experienced in the developmental stage and continue to manifest throughout adulthood: abandonment, separation, rejection, injustice, fear, etc. They are intense wounds that often make us connect with our inner child when we experience conflicts of this type. By connecting with these wounds, we also connect with the unresolved pain of childhood.

Emotion: This is a state of mind that arises in relation to an event, pleasant or unpleasant, and that motivates action. There are primary and secondary emotions. The primary emotions refer to the physiological state that the person experiences about an event. These are divided into two groups, the positive emotions (joy, tranquility) and negative ones (fear, anger, rage, sadness).

Feeling: The stage after an emotion. The feeling is the result of an emotion.

Psyche-brain-organ: This is the relationship between the mind and the organism. This relationship explains how our body acts when the person experiences a conflict and what messages the brain sends to the body. Depending on how we experience a stressful event, our mind (psyche) will interpret what is happening, and the brain will activate the survival mechanisms (flight, paralysis, or attack). Once the moment of conflict is over, our brain will look for a way to discharge residual stress and send a message to an organ related to the biological function of the event experienced. Therefore, we will develop one symptom or another depending on how we have experienced the conflictual event.

Repetitions: These are patterns of behavior and conduct performed in the same way because we have learned that those responses favor survival. If we do not find a solution and discover why we repeat behaviors and conducts, we will consistently achieve the same result. If we learn a new way of coping with stress, we can escape repetition and find internal resources to help us live freely.

Resentment: This is the most visceral sensation, an intense bodily feeling that cannot be put into words. It is the purest emotion.

Resignification: This is the process of giving a new meaning to a traumatic experience so it can be perceived with tranquility once the event has been processed and balance with internal resources has been restored.

Resources: These are strategies that help us regain balance and adapt after a traumatic event. The most powerful resources are internal; we learn to use them to face conflicts, and we can recover from adapting to the situation. https://sentirseamada.com/blog/podcast/tomar-decisiones-dificiles-1/

Ritual, exercise: These are different tools that are used in professional consultation to accompany people in their spiritual process. Rituals serve to connect with the unconscious, allowing us to elaborate duels, close unfinished issues, or resignify a story. https://sentirseamada.com/blog/2020/09/24/ritual-para-alguien-que-termina-una-relacion/

Spiritual accompaniment: This refers to the relationship of cooperation established between an expert (coach, companion) and the person looking for help. A specific process is followed to identify the goals that the patient wants to pursue. Each person has her own pace of accompaniment and is responsible for her own changes. This is why the companion must act in accordance with the patient's needs so as to help her understand the feelings in her body to find a new way of living that is spiritually freer. https://sentirseamada.com/blog/2020/12/07/el-acompanamiento-espiritual-en-el-duelo-por-separacion-para-recuperar-la-alegria-de-vivir/

Stress: Internal or external factors that weaken our body cause us to be more likely to develop new symptoms and have greater difficulty in challenging situations. It is activated when we experience a conflict or when we encounter critical situations. Stress alters our body so much that it forces our brain to exert itself in order to find a solution to restore balance.

Subconscious: According to Carl Jung's studies, the psyche comprises interrelated systems (the conscious – the analytical mind – the individual unconscious, and the collective unconscious). The unconscious stores memories and experiences and manages 97% of our behavior. The subconscious does not distinguish among real, virtual, or imaginary. Therefore, it processes traumatic events quickly.

Symptom: This is a natural mechanism for regaining balance after experiencing a stressful event. It can be physical (such as a stomachache or a fracture), behavioral (psychological traumas, disorders, psychological pathologies that alter our behavior), or existential (when questioning our existence). The symptom is the starting point because it tells us about the conflictual event, its intensity, and the state in which the issue is found.

Thoughts: This refers to the mental reasoning of the intellect. Thoughts are necessary for reason and reflection and form ideas and representations relating to each other.

Transit: This involves walking through the bodily sensations and feeling how they flow and disintegrate until a neutral and balanced state is restored. It is about not blocking an emotion and feeling every sense we perceive.

Trauma: Trauma is a deep emotional wound. It refers to anything that we have experienced from a dramatic event that we have suppressed due to the intensity and shock suffered. The greater the pain of the experience, the greater the trauma and thus its consequences on a physical, mental, and spiritual level.

Visualization: This is relaxation or guided meditation that allows us to connect with the unconscious. Through visualization, we can relax and reduce the intensity of the brain waves. This is achieved by modulating the voice, using a soft, calm, and unhurried tone, and directing each part of the body until a state of relaxation is felt. By relaxing, we can connect with our unconscious and revisit wounds and traumatic experiences. The goal is to see how we feel about something.

Well-being: This is the feeling of emotional fulfillment. The practice of spiritual coaching (reviewing objectives, purpose, goals, and lived experiences, why we act as we do, how we feel in our present, etc.) aims to achieve emotional, physical, and spiritual balance. Well-being is an individual's capacity to reach a state of harmony, calm, and health. It might be different for each person. For this reason, it is crucial to take the time to define what it means for you and how important it is for your health, since health is one of the pillars of well-being.

(1) Natalia Prado. "¿Sueles despertarte a la madrugada? Cada horario tiene su significado y está relacionado con tus órganos y emociones" (May 13th, 2020). BIOGUIA. You can find it at https://www.bioguia.com/entretenimiento/sueles-despertarte-a-la-madrugada-cada-horario-tiene-su-significado-y-esta-relacionado-con-tus-organos-y-emociones_29281228.html

(2) "¿Dormir menos disminuye nuestro coeficiente intelectual?" (May 17th, 2015). Publimetro. From https://www.publimetro.pe.

(3) Correa, Mónica. "6 cosas que están destruyendo tu coeficiente intelectual sin que lo sepas"(May 4th, 2018). La Bioguía. From https://www.bioguia.com

(4) "Nuevas investigaciones sobre el sueño. Prueban que 20 minutos de siesta alcanzan para recuperar la energía." (December 8th, 2016). *Clarín.* From http://www.clarin.com/

(5) You can also find this concept as sleep or heart hygiene.

(6) "La Importancia de conciliar el sueño y descansar en épocas de pandemia" (April 9th, 2020). Alkemy Diagnostico. From: http://www.alkemydiagnostico.com/novedades/noticia/392.

(7) Lucio Villegas "Esta rutina nocturna de 10 minutos te llevará al éxito al día siguiente" (October 27th, 2020). Bioguía.

(8) "La Importancia de conciliar el sueño y descansar en épocas de pandemia" (April 9th, 2020). Alkemy Diagnostico. You can read the full article at http://www.alkemydiagnostico.com/novedades/noticia/392.

(9) "Cómo dormir más esta noche" (April 20th, 2020). *The New York Times.* You can read the full article at https://www.nytimes.com/es/2020/04/02/espanol/estilos-de-vida/insomnio-coronavirus-dormir.html

(10) Cabarrús, Carlos Rafael. *Cuaderno de Bitácora, para acompañar caminantes. Guía psico-histórica- espiritual.* Desclée: Bilbao, 2000, 5th ed. (210-212).

Don't miss out!

Visit the website below and you can sign up to receive emails whenever Yenni Payeski publishes a new book. There's no charge and no obligation.

https://books2read.com/r/B-A-YADQ-RFVRB

BOOKS 2 READ

Connecting independent readers to independent writers.

Also by Yenni Payeski

Problemas para dormir. Rituales y oraciones para que duermas más feliz
Trouble Sleeping? Evolve your spirituality
Acompañamiento espiritual por ruptura amorosa
Descodificación biológica Infantil
BIOLOGICAL DECODING. Children's Books

Watch for more at https://sentirseamada.com/.

About the Author

I am Yenni Payeski. Biological Decoder. Spiritual companion. Life coach. Wife.

Mother. Daughter.

My purpose is to accompany women in discovering the presence of God in their lives, finding HAPPINESS through FAITH and Wellbeing through Biodecoding.

After years of living away from God and my passion for nature, I found in Christianity the best shelter to heal my

wounds. I learned that listening to myself and to others was the way to His infinite love.

Faith led me to become a minister of Silence, Listening, and Reception. In 2016 I founded **Sentirse Amada**, a spiritual center where I offer courses and workshops to help women in their search for well-being through selfknowledge, meditation, and prayer.

With my books, I help you recognize and observe your emotions and give you the tools so you regain trust in yourself and feel the love of God.

Join me at www.setirseamada.com and learn how you can achieve anything you set your heart to!

Read more at https://sentirseamada.com/.

www.ingramcontent.com/pod-product-compliance
Lightning Source LLC
Chambersburg PA
CBHW030806180726
47991CB00024B/1094